A Head Full of Whispers

Peter Langston

ISBN: [978-0-646-57539-1]

Published by Six Nines Imagery
www.sixninesimagery.com

Also by the same author
Six Nines (2009) Kardoorair Press ISBN 978-0-908244-79-9

Whispers.

Did you hear that?
Right up the back there,
hard against the far wall,
long way from sight.

Whispers.

Soft spoken small words,
of direction,
allegation,
suggestion.

Whispers.

Tales of mobs,
country,
hurts,
happiness.

Whispers.

You must have heard that?
Closer now, clearer.
Things I must repeat,
amplify.

My head's full of them.

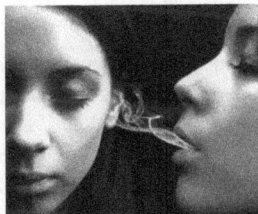

Foreword

It was a great pleasure to be asked to write the foreword to this collection. To say I was daunted, is an understatement, especially in following on a task covered in his first book by the most literary person I know.

It meant that a down to earth, average country bloke has had the chance to read and ponder over some amazing words.

I have known Peter for many years: from earlier teaching days of shared conscientiousness to these later grey and balding times – with him annoyingly and perhaps surprisingly, still having a mass of the hair, despite having had the travails of a legion! To say I know him well would be wrong but I have seen him live through a variety of experiences and times which gives me some background to absorbing the task of reading his work and produce this commentary prefacing it.

When we now stumble on each other through a shared love of cricketing tales or hits of coffee, I am pleasantly thrilled at how happy a place he presents as being in.

I have seen him in various settings and noted his diligence, sincerity, care and passion for education, family, the health of others, fair play, accountability, justice, music, the arts, the environment, his beloved cricket and even his Hawaiian shirts. There are some who may pass judgment over him continuing to wear them. There may even be some he has rankled in some sphere or other as he invariably does things his way - but that is by the by when it comes to this collection.

Approach his poems by accepting some idioms which I think will open your mind. Those who appreciate a good tale well written in a variety of ways fathomable to the common man, will respond "Gee I like that," That's a good one," "Yeah I can picture it," "Wow, that reminds me of" and so on. In "Mangrove Mick" you'll meet a quintessential Aussie. We all know a Mick. I encourage you to read these poems to see Peter and perhaps more importantly, yourselves, in the stories he shares.

It has been an immense pleasure to read such a variety of themes; at various times dark, introspective, reminiscent, immensely romantic, whimsical, critical, sarcastic, sardonic and humorous. These musings are occasionally simplistic but complex enough to have teeth which bite into the reader's consciousness, causing thoughts of shared times, beliefs and feelings. You will smile, wince and cry! I cringed at how close to home some words and phrases were and how much thinking they evoked but rejoiced and was excited about how poems made me recall and talk about times I had forgotten or not remembered at an appropriate time!

Reading on from one to the other and back again allowed the feelings, events and memories he uses to paint pictures all the more intense and made me smile with the thought of others who will read this work and whom I am insisting do so. Do not put this back on the shelf. It is a collection worth pursuing!

There are wordsmiths who will read Peter's work and dissect his style, his use of different literary nuances, how he uses short lines for impact, his foray into rhyme, or the use of self reference and insular thought. Academics can do what they will but for the common man,

I believe this work is just what the doctor ordered – a chance to enjoy and think about life experiences that can make us muse on our own and come into contact with what is being shared. You don't need to be an expert critic to reach the end. Just read the damn thing and soak up the taste, liked or not. Like a new red, announce your opinion from what you taste. In "Coffee For One", he offers a poignant recall of all loss but specifically the loss of self.

My mind resigned a long time ago:
the rest cardboard cut-outs my life,
smiling my own schemes,
building my own scaffolds.
The bits of me left
missing the bit that left,
on another grey, wet day.

This is a series of poems that you can read and work with, at whatever level you find. The range of phrases and how they are used, constantly thrilled me. In "Empty" there's the old man ignored by his family

dull eyes
and stories,
learned for loved ones,
wasted on strangers

Criticism of past poets, including Peter, who write in a style supposed to be too insular or personal, astounds me. I have always thought that the best writing comes from the shared experience. In "Mona Lisa's Secret" he expresses amazing love in the simple act of having coffee but holds back the mystery of any relationship

We smile the years
holding hands by fingertip over coffee
and she tells me Mona Lisa's secret.

I certainly don't want to go back to university days to analyse and judge works I read now and I trust other readers will try this collection for nothing more than to enjoy a contemporary Aussie wordsmith, willing to bare his soul and expose what has molded him.

Peter has been forthright and most open about where he has been and is - from discussions on the radio to guest appearances at community groups - and this collection will be a terrific lift for those who want to face whatever is over their shoulder : the shadows or the light. In "Walking Tall Hurts" his line *I stoop experience* describes us all: the young under the pressures of today and their forefathers. Even if you have *rebuilt after storm damage* you have to keep getting up and do the tall walking.

You are now one of those with the chance to pick up this work and take some time over it.

The message from one like me, famous for going from the back pages first, is to 'suck it and see'.

Enjoy.

Barry Everingham

Contents

Whispers About People

"*The world needs its poem-whisperers; those who can charm the things out of words.*"
Chris Mansell, from "Letters"

3 Gens Fishing

beating
beating
beating
beating

    washing in
    washing out
    washing in
    washing out

        nothing changes

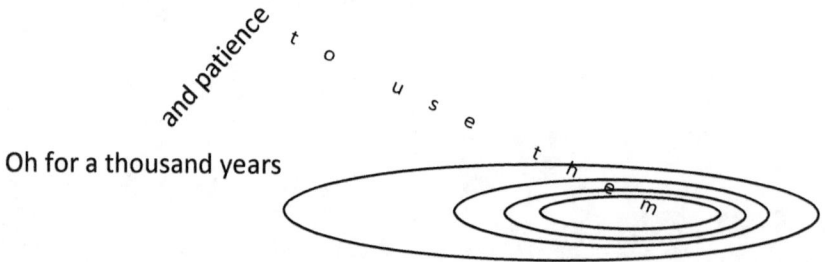

            cunjevois open and shut
            seagulls hop about
            sootie oystercatchers nitpick
            the water pounds
            the rocks remain
            so it has been
            as sons of sons of fathers
            stand fishing tied lifetimes

                nothing changes

and patience *t* *o* *u* *s* *e*

Oh for a thousand years

t *h* *e* *m*

8

Mangrove Mick

He's teaching there on his small white boat,
where the mozzies are large and thick.
At that meeting place of salt and fresh,
bare-foot Mangrove Mick.

As the mangroves sip on Daintree Soup,
he shares all their breeding tricks.
Naming birds by sound and snakes by sight,
bare-foot Mangrove Mick.

Sensing newbie's with such thirsty minds,
he shows them how to drink.
Painting his home with a bushie's brush,
bare-foot Mangrove Mick.

In barely three Daintree hours,
what's shared is encyclopaedia thick,
till at day's end the egrets land,
to a silent Mangrove Mick.

White birds land thousands strong,
an invitation offered at a flick.
From strangers to friends, meeting minds,
with bare-foot Mangrove Mick.

If you ever thirst at the Daintree River
needing something your brain can lick;
if your senses hunger for the cycle of life,
look up bare-foot Mangrove Mick.

Empty

A shake,
no,
a tremor,
no,
a shake,
There,
in his hand,
as his coffee shudders
to his mouth.
Unintended drips
trickling into hiding places
on an ancient, bearded chin.

Eyes dulled by years
of seeing too much
and tears for loves lost;
friends past
and lives
too soon forgotten.
No more stories
or reflections
for grandchildren
who outgrew lessons,
stealing their noise back
from rooms he made for them.

Just a shake,
dull eyes
and stories,
learned for loved ones,
wasted on strangers
and no longer wanted.

He Never Knew

He never knew what chances we took
before planning his conception.

He never knew that joy and fear
are bundled emotional software.

He never knew our ignorance
put him on a pre-birth precipice.

He never knew I just stopped breathing
when his first wriggle explored my love.

He never knew what we never had
so he could have everything.

He never knew I wanted to catch him
at every teenage fall.

He never knew the bills we paid
so his independence escaped illusion.

He never knew of my bloated pride
when mates chaired him from success.

He never knew of smiling tears
disguised on his graduation day.

He never knew of a pacing father
listening for a taxi's slamming door.

(He never knew ...)
A blue light taxi's slamming door
(... he never knew.)
Sir, I regret to inform you ...

I never told him.

Finding Radames

Superlatives spill uncensored from reckless lips,
hasty praise overstating adjectives,
promoting unearned greatness
in these days of careless compliment.
Middle age slows our pace,
thickens waist and thigh
but gifts perspective
and values credibility.

I don't want to live like that

From this safer place,
I sit in darkness,
pensive and observant,
that I might not miss
the chance to justify my pride:
as if my judgment
could alter facts by passion.

I don't want to love like that

I hear his booming bass,
one ear turned, tuned
to the partnership of noted friends,
the rest joined to a brother
singing our hearts open.
Songs as stories
told new again,
honey thick but crystal clear,
by bright eyed custodians
now in their time.
Moving in spotlight white,
all red and gold,
he seduces me
as all stars will.

Sparkling against surroundings
which have thrust him up
to shine for love lost,
now as then,
to bring me forward
from my lonely full house seat
immersed in love's uncompromising conflict.
Singing me past pages,
tingling soft touches
feather brush where beauty waits,
veiled by masculinity's disadvantage,
to brink its brim
and wash me with his vocal tap,
clean of wasted days,
so I can celebrate my luck,
return to my brick veneer realm
and find her waiting,
heart open,
for her Radames.

Self Portrait of a Difficult Pleasure

The most fundamental reason one paints is in order to see ... +

... what did you see?
Did eyes stained by colour notice beige carpet
insipid curtains indistinct in tired cream
a sallowed bathroom, sanitised for your protection?
Did red bricks draw you in,
colour blind on smack,
where they knew you by name,
not reputation ...

... what did you see?
Needles and horse for clarity.
Fearing death, you died by proxy,
still wanting life
trying to convict us
in your genius
urging our belief
in the oldest boy's self portrait ...

... what did you see
as that final, pure flood climbed your arm?
Sensual lines struggling to border vermilion?
Boneless hips and accessible intimacy,
a hunger you fed the world?
Lavender Bay boats and birds and blues:
saturations of ultramarine,
songs of Wendy ...

Everyone reaches a point in their life where they must either change or cease.+

... where did you go
to escape Thirroul's Room 4?
Paris, where seduction beguiled every breath?
Sofala, where light obscured colour?
London, where Arkie was born among brushes?
New York, where you realised The American Dream?
Fiji, where birdies fluttered to your canvas?
or Surry Hills on a Sunday afternoon ...

... who did you see
as colour and line and light faded to faces?
Were Dylan, Elenberg or Patrick there?
Did Christie covert your blue veined hand?
Did you beg undergiveness
of Arkie or Wendy or even Brett?
Who stayed to light a candle?
Matisse, Van Gogh, Modigliani, Bacon?

I put my heart and my soul into my work and have lost my mind in the process*

... was your best unpainted
in this restless search,
this difficult pleasure?
This gift, this birthright,
did you tune it
enlarge it?
Did you protect and share it?
That gift ... that infliction.

You draw me here,
within a brush stroke,
every line a honey trap,
your soul in Pandora's care.
Mad curls in Indian ink,
stamps of calligraphic homage
and neat precise eyes,
drawn, not painted ...

... Dibbs volunteer prisoner,
we held hands with brush and pen
until our gifts, our pleasures
exhausted me in tears
for an appetite unsated.
All I have are words,
by tool and choice,
impotent by comparison.

*Cheat and deceive and lie and exaggerate and most particularly distort ... and you'll
see something you've never seen before and that is the beginning of yourself and that
heralds the beginning of difficult pleasure.+*

15

12 Bar Revenge

she leaves
      He's hurt
she laughs
      He's curt

she mocks
He thinks
she flaunts
He drinks

her next
His mate
she scoffs
His fate

she's gone
His guitar
her damage
Twelve bars

her deceit His shame
Simple verse Repeats again
Sounding bell   Warning brings
Crying song   Sobbing strings
Their life   Torn apart
Addled head Trespassed heart
Pick out chords Where the pain will be
Weep His story   Am   G   F   C
Let him be Thrum the fretting
No japing here Blues to sing
Blues to sing

Cuppa and Conversations Before Play
(For Peter)

I'm sitting above ghosts
of action past
and yet to come.
45 minutes hence
white heroes will emerge
on checks of green,
focused in the nation's lens
from every angle,
in colour and infrared.
Sharing a cuppa,
thinking on the game,
he sits with me,
one moment trapped in *hasha*
the next whimsical
channelled by an *chenjera*
rarely seen in the public seats.
The Gabba imitates our lives:
one side colour and humanity
the other screaming silent, lonely *kungura* .
We stand for a minute
as old men recall an Invincible Sam
for grandsons asking who.
In the cold, white, early Brisbane glare
his *kurukura* is warm,
spoken or written.
I'm forced to think,
released to smile
... until a *ndemo mhepo* ruffles my pages
and he is gone,
straw hat bobbing in the colours.
Swallowed by his complexity
a camouflage of language
revealing only a *manzvinzvidza*
from within his forever fortress.

Temp(er)est

I caught the edge of it,
that storm I failed to predict,
which blew through the kitchen last night.
I heard the last thunderclaps
and was splashed by the final shower,
as you left,
your mother's love
rung out by your hands,
as an old towel might be
after sopping up storm damage,
till twisted and twisted,
it flops,
spent,
damp but no longer sodden
and of no further use.

Such damage you carelessly left,
with the unconcern
only youthful selfishness condones.
No consolation for the storm damaged.
I might brush off spots,
where she remains inundated,
flood scars beyond the high tide mark,
but your anger makes silt,
who's marks can be removed …
… but not the smell.
I wonder,
how long will you need to do this,
before you build levies,
to protect yourself?

Man-O-War/Pause

Your fugue,
erupting from calm waters,
tossed waves under me,
over me,
splashed hate in burning droplets,
acid wash,
never intended
for treasures
or the nurtured few.
Where were the warning clouds?
The rolling claps of caution?
What forecast did I neglect?
Safer courses
sometimes miss their destinations,
so when fug buys vowels,
I baton down
and ride your fury,
till sunshine finds reason
and me,
again,
waiting ,
with a cautious smile.

This Afternoon In The Library

This afternoon in the library
when I was too scared to go home,
or too sensible,
I took my watching post
and scribbled unimportant lines, importantly,
while you played in children's books.

You ran past my melancholy,
all gasping excitement and questions,
leaving Mummy in your wake
with a brother on wheels
and a sister patted under Mother's hand,
sucking on umbilical love.

I saw you clap hands,
first on each other, then either cheek,
as sparkling eyes became drunk with books.
Watched you leap to hug Mummy
in thanks and unbridled bliss.
Saw you spring at the shelves.

Your arms grabbed random bundles.
Little legs staggered backward to bean bag heaven
and the frenzy started.
In the ten minutes whilst a brother settled,
too young to be insatiable for words and pictures,
you had a bedroom cupboard of questions.

Somehow, despite your sister's bulky intrusion,
Mummy curled around you,
took her first born to that place
where he will always have sanctuary
and listened and answered and smiled
and warmed herself on your imagination.

I watched you there,
so honest in your wonder
and ate regret in thick slices
at fifty years of forgetting,
forgetting how it is to be you.
Dreams yet to be slept on.

You left,
skipping treasures past me.
Stopping, head to one side in judgment,
you passed me fit, smiled
and showed me your book.
I've been smiling tears since.

This afternoon in the library
I found a reason.

I'll Say It Then

I have mumbled it.
I have shown it.
I have shouted it.
I have cried it often.
I write it now
to start a new journey,
grateful to see your footprints
beside mine, beside yours.
The bright sunshine
casts no shadows
and sends monsters
over our shoulders,
banished by our choice,
behind us,
where we need not look.

Closer,
the horizon,
all sweet dreams
and fields unploughed.
Watch my smile,
feel yours burning.
Can two hearts syncopate feeling?
One thought be cherished
in two different minds?

Let's run ourselves breathless.
We'll pant and smile,
sweat from us every good thing
we had a right to enjoy.
I'll say it
then,
when life could get no better ...

... and watch your eyes improve it.

Mona Lisa's Secret

I'm s t r e t c h i n g thoughts out to dry,
words borrowed from others
as scaffold for my own context.
Watching them dry,
take shape into your meanings,
different than I wrote them.
Writing in the sunshine before muesli.
Paul Kelly and a balcony by the sea.
Bright sun and breakfast cereal.

An apparition joins me
reads my random thoughts
and smiles a lifetime in an instant,
all smooth skin and pared back years.
If I squint,
if I think,
if I conjure,
what thirty years have bought us,
not taken away,
she is still my best moments.
We smile the years,
holding hands by fingertip over coffee
and she tells me Mona Lisa's secret.

When She Smiles

... and when she smiles
the moon goes dull,
the sun hides
and seeks
the company
of clouds
or passing planets.
Both escape comparison.
Her eyes tell tales
tall and sweet.
Her mouth
makes corners
which twitch messages
of acceptance and invitation.
Both sparkle,
one breathes a kiss
passing through conversations,
across a room,
to find my cheek
blushed and tingled
and alive with the memory
of every touch ...

... and when she laughs ...

Whispers About Places

*"Every blade of grass has its angel that
bends over it and whispers ... grow, grow."*

The Talmud

The Coorong, Mate

Just got back from the Coorong mate,
where the Murray used to flow.
Now it can't breech the sandbars mate,
the way it used to go.

The birds are crying at the Coorong mate.
Their food has all been had.
Without a regular flowing mate,
the lakes have all gone bad.

It's going dry at the Coorong mate,
a salt scum forms a sheet.
The mouth is shallow and narrow mate
and barely two feet deep.

Everywhere you look in the Coorong mate,
the past has gone to die ...
but the sea floods into marinas mate
and the rich boys boats ride high.

On the way down there to the Coorong mate,
I stopped where everything grew.
Where fruit and wine all tasted great,
but the Murray was greenish blue.

I reckon if you love the Coorong mate,
if you love the Murray too,
perhaps it's time for a quiet word,
before polliegators screw you too.

I just got back from the Coorong mate,
where the Murray used to flow.
It can't breech the sand at the river mouth,
the way it used to go
in a wide, brown muddy flow.
How much more do you need to know?

10 Minutes In Nth Qld

The air, pregnant with rain,

gives late afternoon birth,

as bush thick knees sing the songs of their fathers

in celebration of broken tension.

A chorus of friends join in

as Ringo-drops beat on corrugated drums.

A breeze stirs the wet curtain,

committing sweat to history

on bare backs and smile-scarred faces.

One face, work-stained but worry free,

looks up and drinks in mad lapped slurps,

his yellow and orange work camouflage

clings soaked to tired muscles.

From a doorway,

a smile and nod is shared,

as I stare into the big, fat rain

and colours as bold as any manic day.

idea

Binna Burra Sunrise

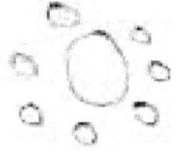

I'm crowded by my solitude,
sitting in this rainforest clearing,
watching an old habit repeat itself
for the second trillionth time.
A new sun rises,
dressed in orange pyjamas,
surprised to find me watching
its early morning stretches.
It might be a lonely view,
so high,
so far from home
and things I can find in the dark,
but I wear my brother's beanie,
a champion's shield.
I hide inside a cable knit,
each stitch my mother's love.
I have my father's smile.

Tree tops catch the Sun's first throws,
standing on broad tip toes,
waving thousands of fingers
to draw its golden attention.
A brazen crow lands noisily,
all flap and bother and complaint,
then gargles and clears his throat
with celebrated obscenity.
A strangler's embrace
on a tiring beech,
an unbalanced love affair
two hundred years to the death.

Lewin's sweet tooth flutters about:
bottlebrush takeaway - flies with that?
Whipbirds crack and chatter,
telling the bush of their love.
A carpet snake, fat on antechinus,
hides from the night in the rockery .
A restless brush turkey shifts and scratches,
never satisfied, like a remote controlling teen.

The wind whistles a familiar tune.
Bush sounds sing in chorus,
in herald,
in celebration.
These Maker's labels
wave understanding
at the last creation.
Evidence to its doubt,
vibrancy to blindness
and redemption still on offer.
Binna Burra greets the sun.
An unanticipated friend,
bearing gifts,
accepted.

Iluka Bluff

Sitting below Iluka Bluff,
its ramparts against the moody sea,
our backrest in the sunshine.
The sneaky sea,
all smiles and gentle waves,
that eat the rock platform,
with a billion year old hunger,
takes only small bites today.

Like the bulwark at our backs,
shielding sand dune and rainforest
from an untameable enemy,
you sit beside me,
in the same instant
weathered and beautiful,
strong and soft,
damaged yet complete.

My weatherproof wonder wall,
you kept other dangers at bay,
while storms engulfed me
and a sea of madness
flooded my lowest ground,
rising me to toe tips for breath,
until, breathing the blackness yourself,
your constant grip effected my rescue.

Here in the sunshine of our rocky seats,
with gulls as our playful company,
and small creatures swaying their precarious lives
in shallow, intermittent pools of reds and greens,
I note the past for challenges overcome,
but linking fingers, we talk the future,
a song we have always sung
when our hearts are happiest.

We talk for hours,
pausing only to laugh or kiss.
We talk through apples and sultanas,
low flying jets and high flying dolphins.
So crowded in our isolation,
on our rocky platform.
Scaring the sea into repeated retreat,
from the completeness of our love.

In Steel Rudd's Pub

Dad & Dave and even Mabel,
sang their myths of country life,
from a pint pot in a writer's hand,
in Steel Rudd's pub,
at his own selection,
in a rough cut bar,
a fettler's thirsty glance
from Nobby Siding.
Where the Darling Downs
run south to old enemies,
where obtuse Aussie humour
calls redheads blue,
it names this flat land Nobby.
Halving the distance
between then and now,
Sister Kenny unpolioed polio,
even straightening dogs hind legs,
with determination and hot rags ...
... yep, right here mate.

Today at the pub,
three men and a dog
pass afternoon verdict
on anything:
solving big problems slowly,
with small ideas
and opinions dried by humour,
then freshly wet
with pots of gold,
at the end of the rainbow.
Sunset lights old angles,
its red/orange slant on history,
firing imaginations
four generations after Rudd
painted his bush characters

from dream into archetype.
I wander through his story,
dining on Guiness rich pie,
surrounded by Nobby's ghosts,
calling me in black and white,
contented at their times,
in tall timber buildings
burned to the ground a frame later.
Cars my father drove,
stand as handsome company
to the new General Store,
while in neighbouring frames,
ladies in long white dresses,
hiding seven petticoats,
stand improbably on dusty streets,
in the Qld heat,
smiling.
Soldiers pose without returning.
Dogs dance and bark.
Black men,
not named then,
are unknown still.
47 kids dressed from pinafore to penniless
and 1 straight backed teacher.
All noted, detailed and catalogued,
in meticulous hand,
each one an incendiary device,
for a story longing a spark.

Here history hangs
for Rotary dinner guests,
who never notice.
Steel Rudd's words made famous,
while these forgotten faces stare,
in strange adoration,
at the passing parade,
on its way to the bar.

Goodbye In Townsville

I took my farewells to Castle Hill
to watch you pass by,
to your new cloudy neighbourhood.
I waved,
even sent you a long tearful kiss,
knowing the next one
would have to cross half Australia.
I withheld a sob,
but not a second one
or a third.

Dawn flushed your plane
all pinks and reds.
I didn't see you wave,
but imagined you:
the last-loaded,
testing breathing
and ignoring pain.
Playing with memories,
pieces of me
gone with you,
to keep you safe.

New tears found me
as you found clouded space,
asked for coffee,
the sound of home
growing in your ears.
All I heard,
down the steep descent
which started my slower trip,
was the tedious kiss
of rubber on road
and the doubts of following days,
teasing me forward.

Moonrise at Emu Park

A fat yellow moon,
plump with romance's suggestions,
rises from it's Pacific bath,
warm and drip dry.
It's reflection runs to me,
straight broken steps,
an imperfect set of moving yellow dashes,
a zebra crossing of small steps
and giant leaps.
A seagull calls the last youngster to sleep.
A dolphin surfaces,
blows,
then dives in a slow, lazy arc.
The singing ship whispers secrets,
tales I've never heard
but know by heart.
The same breeze brushes past,
touching my cheek
with lady fingers,
making tears cling cold
and stop in their tracks.

The Emu left long ago.
Echoes of Darumbal dreaming,
have become a nightmare
of caravans on pensions
and corpulent kids spoiled by guilt
and the rapists who wring it dry ...
... except in the dark,
on this point,
tonight.
The last couple nod goodnight,
one merged entity after kisses
and promises made
on a fat yellow moon.

Byron Bay

Cars nudge each other,
frustrated by inevitability,
overheated by cool pedestrians
and a lack of parking spaces.
The beautiful people,
apparently immune to irony,
wander and stand about.
Malibu facsimiles of vague humanity.

Breasts bounce an oiled defiance,
of age, gravity and social mores.
Screw me hips and fuck you expression,
mixed scents off brown babe bodies
promenading temptation and control.
Sexual chocolates who demand respect,
claiming their social wages
without doing the work.

Post-feminist programming,
pre-feminist chassis.
Penis fly traps,
self-demeaned by trend adherence.
Slinking behind latest shades,
in designer you name it,
on sun stretched skin.
Come here, come here, go away.

The might be men one day,
strut in the safety of herds,
growling scorn and ridicule
at new bulls in the paddock.
Shirts lost and sun sneaking revenge.
Branded by exposed waistband elastic.
Ink snarling obscenity.
Literate biceps but empty mouths.

Eyes in the top of their head,
protected by sunglasses.
A second, pin-holed set
catalogue last night's atrocities,
effortlessly dismissed.
Muscles ripple warnings.
Perfection is admitted by nods and nudges
at passing cars and even women.

Little brown bodies
with dope coloured names
bounce and run,
theirs' the only innocence.
No hat or shirt or 30+.
No worries or sense,
just investments
in a skin specialist's future holiday.

Turned on, tuned in, dropped out ...
... beautiful people,
all care, no responsibility.
Leaving Harmony or Storm
in the wake of adult choices,
to run wild in bare feet,
whilst "first name basis" parents
fry skin, brains and social liability.

My car finally goes nose in,
a Roadstar and panel van for neighbours,
as breasts bounce by,
and sunglasses perv
at generations disappearing
in melanomic smoke,
masked by a familiar sickly smell,
while I drink coffee ...

... one morning in Byron Bay.

Counting Cowboys

More Saturday night egos
than real singing stars.
A lot less Queenslanders
wet in their cars.

1000's of strangers
with sun raw faces.
300 long arms
in unlawful places.

100's of big hats
on rough headed guys.
74 denim pockets
flapping on thighs.

30 loud amps
deafening Peel St.
The 25 dumbest
people you'll meet.

14 times Kenny
played gambler's fool.
11 pm people
in next door's pool.

10 old muttons
pretending at lamb.
9 times the Lights
came over to damn.

8 singing noses
Were Not Pretty Enough.
7 broke into yodels
as if calling my bluff.

6 inmates of Folsom
heard the whistling train.
5 days of heat/rain
no courtesy remains.

4 different steps in boot scoot
(who would have guessed).
4 cops on bikes
smiling for cutie's no less.

3 obnoxious brats
stars in their dad's spin.
2 buskers worth paying
amongst all the din.

1 angry storm
but a river in banks.
1 monumental stuff up
but Lee still said thanks.

No decent parking spots
and the traffic is slow.
It's over, stop counting,
355 days to go.

The Water Hole - 1

He came to watch them swim;
tall bodies,
short bodies,
white or faded
and mostly plump.
All ages
and stages
of disregard
for the story of this place.
It's purpose,
not for them,
stolen by them.
They splashed in sunshine,
braved the rain,
laughing little screams,
screaming little laughs,
mostly swimming badly
to where the deep water
sent them shivering
to the shallows,
with cold
or fear
or both.

The Water Hole - 2

She swam alone at sunset.
The first day,
shedding her skin neatly,
wading near the edges
and easily spooked to the shore.
On the second,
she entered with naked grace,
gently working arms and feet,
till only toes touched sand
and face the air.
On her third
confident day,
he took an easy breath,
dropped eyes into the green,
swished his tail
and feasted.

39

Sunshine & Shadows

Sunshine, bright for an April day,
lights and shades the vertical faces,
and lonely sentinels standing offshore,
whose silent warning
is only apparent in calm seas
on clear, blue and yellow days,
when dangers are murmured
and death seems remote
when glanced from behind a barrier.
Humanity is chattering today in the sunshine.
Recording awe in point & shoot megapixels.
Comments accented by Asia and America.
Laughing and smiling their way back to the bus,
after sharing the frame with your timeless danger,
standing almost benign in the sunshine.

In fog and darkness and rain and wind,
120 years of yesterdays and an angry sea before,
two miles offshore Captain Gibson,
a blind man with no stick,,
has made judgments which are twenty miles wrong
and dead-reckoned the Loch Ard and her lives
to an approaching death.
Even at this distance, 200 feet of welcome
pulses panic through his sea bones.
"All hands" is the call and hands, arms, backs respond
too late to change their course
or history's parallel charter.
Wooden bow and beam are no match
and Mutton Birds gaze quizzically as she splinters,
gifting the sea both innocent and guilty.

Watching the white foam swirl and hunt for home
at the narrow gash where land meets sea,
a three foot swell surges and goes in all directions,
to hidden rocks and their razor barnacles,
to sheer cliff walls where handholds disappear,
and back to me,
standing on this gritty golden sand,
warm and wet through my toes.

Dry above the sea which reaches for me,
I put the roar behind me,
stare in their cave,
look up the fortress walls above,
where my old travelling companion waves
like the culturally correct beside her.
I hope I can manage the stairs.

English and Irish voices screaming,
in sounds shaped by every age,
from an old man's anguish to an infant's cry.
The sea drowns them, punishes their audacity,
their husks floating up for days on lonely beaches,
for gulls and bigger birds to pick over.
Tom who had swum from a wreck before
and threaded that narrow gap in a twenty foot swell,
lay spitting the sea from stomach and lungs
on the gritty, wet sand, somehow safe.
Death, standing by, called him through Eva's voice,
seventeen, terrified, freezing,
crying him back to the sea.
The mystery, not that he went but that they returned,
to shelter in a cave's darkness till God appeared at dawn.

I climb the wooden stairs, controlling my asthmatic breathing,
Tom stretched each exhausted finger and toe for holds
pausing on a platform to consider the scene.
Too scared fear would take him with a look down
Cresting the stairs, Sue's eyes smile her love.
Below, the passenger Eva might die of cold or grief
On the short walk back we share hands and a joke.
Tom set out, running from some reserve no one has
At the car we kiss, soaked in pleasure
running to the light twelve miles away
and parcelled in this safety, we drive on
'till Tom led his team of rescuers back.
to other wonders and photo opportunities.
Eva's family died on the Loch Ard.
Tom's future sons all died at sea.

I see things in the shadows in the bright sunlight.
Do you?

Monet's Garden

Monet was in my garden last night,
left brush strokes everywhere
and like the honeyeaters and bees,
I'm feasting this morning.
Two Silvereyes dart past
but stop to agree with me
at red bottlebrush elevenses.
Wide spread grapevine leaves
splatter me with shade
that a voracious passionfruit missed.
Kangaroos Paws hop with the breeze.
Blackbirds go cleaning among weeded soil.
A Fairy Wren couple take youngsters shopping.
A Friarbird chuckles among the pollen
and Sparrows gossip on the lawn.
Colours everywhere:
reds, yellows, pinks, whites.
Greens in all.
If I squint through my cataract eye,
a little footbridge shimmers dimly
and a stream idles by,
as I paint my words,
in Monet's garden.

Whispers About Me

"I must be guilty of something … just whisper it in my ear."

Bob Dylan, "Tight Connection To My Heart"

Study

Sun is up.
My study satiates on light.
Streeton's light.
No room for shadows,
just sweet voices
calling through the window,
warning the worms
and
sweeter ideas,
warming my heart.

There's a Black Dog,
in a far off corner,
of a distant paddock,
cowering,
whimpering.
Serves you right,
you atramentous bastard.

Coffee For One

Grey, wet day,
just outside the glass,
leeching the colour from me,
any enthusiasm soaked
to a soggy set of useless ideas.
Wish I had someone
to laugh with over coffee,
instead of grinning politicians,
TV-lying to make me happy.
Smiles hide schemes.
A simple rise of an eyebrow
consigns me to a second hand bin.
A glance can kill and
a comment can be epitaph.

Rooted through,
bargain hunters
seek my gifts,
to write letters for B causes;
to reclaim memories from microfilm
for histories no one will read;
to minute meeting drivel;
to write shopping lists.

My mind resigned a long time ago:
the rest cardboard cut-outs my life,
smiling my own schemes,
building my own scaffolds.
The bits of me left
missing the bit that left,
on another grey, wet day.

Coffee for one it seems.

Today Is For Crying

Words find hiding places:
in mirth
or public affairs
or coming events
or
silence,
punctuating grief like a careless axe,
wounds of misplaced need,
theirs over yours.

Society engages grief briefly,
needs it over,
soon, soon, soon.
Friends offer cumbersome kindness.
The best let touch speak,
hugging and listening the demons away
at your chosen time
at your chosen pace
and soak tears
on broad shoulders,
honouring loans once given,
by faithful others.

Walking in treacle,
life marches on
around you,
without you,
outside your door ...

... where the sun still rises
and despite contrary certainty,
joy looks us up
and calls in for a cup of tea.

Happiness,
that long-time houseguest,
is found sitting in the corner,
forgotten,
smiling,
not sure why she was ever lost.

Breaths become moments
and moments minutes,
till minutes police the beat
to a regular rhythm
and even pain becomes tolerable.
The best in us rises.

But not yet.
Today is still for crying.

Anniversary

I didn't miss you yesterday.
Found no poignant moment
in photo albums
or shared stories.
Fondled no memories
from knick-knacks.
Drew no pain of absence
to the surface,
where it hid in the privacy
of cherished conversations.
I didn't imagine your smile,
your shaking hand,
your sparkling eyes
or half finished cups of tea.
I devised no schemes
for crying,
to drain and flush,
to heal,
to pacify,
to justify a mother's love
and a still sad son.

I did none of those things.
I took the day off,
using this anniversary
like others treat
each day since you died.

I'll miss you again tomorrow.

Respect

You tell your lies with a casual reality.
Belief suspended so often,
with such dreadful clarity,
you no longer question the sincerity gap.

Enveloped in security you once deserved,
you survive on borrowed credibility,
family respecting the whole,
disgusted by the black hearted part.

You'll rape this falsehood.
Suck it dry like your other discards.
Shrugging your shoulders till sunset
and bulldusting your innocence.

I'll keep my slanders private.
Holding my best from you,
painting laughter on a mask.
Leaving respect at home.

Missing Joni Mitchell

I'm lost in your churning jaws,
grinding and flapping
like line-hung tea-towels
abused by the wind,
as Extra dodges molars.

"Can I help ya?"
rolled over black glossed lip,
jagged upward on an invisible hook.
Wide eyes below a painted monobrow
burn holes in my pause.
The vast experience of her 19 years
now at my disposal.

Still mesmerised by her chewing gums,
I eventually divulge a purpose.
Behind the chest high counter
and wide screen monitor,
I am granted an identity,
and retreat.
Here in the echoes of an Anglican manse,
where bishops conjured theology,
I wait for my psychiatrist,
partitioned by his last line of defence
from the crazies in waiting.
She has too much gum, too much skin
and not enough years or neckline.
Around me,
other madmen wait.
Monet,
Lautrec,
Lawson
and even Vincent,
chuckling in words and brush strokes.

We all behave.
Reading old gossip,
breathing away anxieties,
watching fellow wild beasts
trapped in the bent mind spotlight.
We catalogue each other's oddities.
Trapped here in turbulent indigo,
no one's pissing in fireplaces today.

The Lies That Bind

Sunday morning:
pancakes, coffee, conversation.
I'm caught between redemption and sunshine.
Bread crumbs and bad wine or ...
bird calls and breaths of new air.
Trained to worship one way, their way,
guilt greets alternate paths to heaven.
Guilt, responsibility, shame,
passengers on these carriages I've chosen,
apparently,
yet the forgiveness I read of,
seems free of such intense obligations,
asks only for faithful loyalty.
Automatic membership of The Club,
transfers my ownership to others
who seek to own my thoughts,
my decisions,
even my words.
Ownership unearned by other's promises,
at a watery cross,
on my crying infant head,
before I could say no.
They hold forgiveness like stiff plastic,
flashed at heaven's gate.
They crave it,
desire it,
lust for it,
and call themselves Christ's men.
Christian.

The sun was warm.
Birds voiced sweet melodies.
I walked an hour,
free to think,
floating closer to you
than structured months have allowed.
Unburdened of symbols and liturgy,
selfishly shaped to replicate shallow reflections,
ordering my heart-strung connection
into others' rows,
'till no seats are left for Him.

I walked,
away and back again.
Whispered our conversation.
Kept some of it for later.
It was a good Sunday.

Walking Tall Hurts

Now I'm old enough
to stand on my own two feet,
my knees hurt,
my back aches.
I stoop experiences,
walk chapters of Dickens.

Yet,
I survived my children,
outlasted Dad's advice,
achieved enough,
rebuilt after storm damage,
re earned respect.

But walking tall hurts,
even on sunny days,
with a blue green sea
chasing white beanies,
and tickly toed children laughing
as birds sing to an ocean backbeat.

Down my street,
the dangers lurk,
down every street,
round every corner.
Die those 1000 deaths,
or walk tall,

even though it hurts

The End

The end will come at indecent pace.
When it does, hold back your tears.
Keep those salty clouds 'till later days,
for as breath leaves and lips parch,
I want to breath you as my last gulps,
drink the smile in your eyes.
My life was pregnant with words,
some wasted in haste,
so hold the best of them,
and brag to the world in aftermath.
As I leave, lock eyes with me.
Talk of love from those abundant wells.
Pour your soul into me,
ticketing my destination.
Touch me with your best caress,
that I might feel your warmth
sending me on my way.
Wish me well from memory
of sunny days and laughter
and bonds as strong as a gentle touch.
Leave me with your image,
held behind last closed lids.

Only then,
cry your oceans,
but tell the world
what you have lost
and talk in funny parables,
lengthy and grin-smartingly funny,
of who I was,
not might have been,
and of our love.

Silent Night

The ghosts of Christmas past
are sharing stories in the silent hours
in this capacious, empty house.
Drinking chamomile in place of youthful potions,
I listen to their anecdotes
of post-bedtime parental intrigue,
when these adults who'll come to breakfast
once woke at daylight,
convinced of false truths
and eyes sparkling
with hope untarnished.

These vapours of past Decembers
recall secret bed frames,
passed through windows,
as soft-curled sleepy heads
drew long breaths in protected kip.
Or building blocks sanded past midnight
by a mother's hands,
not long past their own childhood,
into safe-edged shapes
for little fingers and a big imagination
to strum into life.

These phantoms from among the tinsel
offer me gifts before this new Holy dawn.
A soft smile, a warm tear,
a heart so brimmed with belonging
that a small tan dog with white stockings
is as clear as two brothers
talking life in quiet retreat;
sons spilling wine in a mother's glass
or on a white table cloth;
and a daughter ringing home,
a woman laughing love like a little girl.

With heralds still to hark
these happy spectres leave me smiling,
lingering for boys
who looked like men at 3:00 am.
Waiting for them to come
and colour in my fading spaces
with brushes sopped in memories.
I greet dawn like it's my secret;
talk soft words with the missing
by a plastic tree dangling stories
cloaked as children's ornaments.

Belief dabs freedom on my heart.

The Silent Room

too much guilt too much blame
too many unspoken accusations
smiled over the gap between us
an eternity of thought
I'm disalloweD
a Broken Arm
of thE body
Of ChriSt
It's His faulT
He made me thinK
encouraged me to speaK
in a silent room of strangerS

When Dougie Did The Double

Summer blazed in grainy black & white,
until I walked through a TV window
past stands of old corrugated iron and older wood,
into the vivid colours of my youth
and found a new home between
the Randwick and Paddington ends.
White skins were pink and brown
and black came in different shades
as a battle between willow and leather
made the sounds of resonant gun shots
across an oval billiard table
of deep green, light green mown magic.
I passed my first Test watching a first.
National service done but, he still stood to attention
to clip laconically to leg or pull with surprising violence
and all recorded in scribbled tallies
in the vacant back pages of 6th class maths.
Such days, such firsts
never to be repeated
never to be forgotten.
Heroes dressed as heroes are,
all stains and flaws lost in the whiteness,
all the same, all different,
all heroes through twelve year old senses
fresh to colour and sounds and smells
too big to imagine or rich to swallow
without savouring the sensation.
Cut grass aromas new just now;
a bobbing towelling hat mosaic
in hues so bright I still squint;
the cheering politeness to both victor and vanquished;
and a crowd wit still entertaining
down this winding corridor of years.
Wonders not lost on an aging boy's spirit.
I was there.
I still am.

Poet's Notes

Page 9: Mick was our guide on a Daintree River cruise. By our, I mean the two of us. He asked us what we wanted to see and we replied "what you want to show us.". Somehow we soaked in an ecosystem in those four hours, finishing in the rain, watching thousands of cattle egrets flying in to roost at sunset.

Page 12: my eldest is a talented singer who played the lead in Aida; his younger brother a talented musician

Page 14: quotes in italics by Brett Whiteley (+) and Vincent van Gogh (*). This poem was selected for the "1000 Words Exhibition" at the New England Regional Art Museum in 2011. It was written in response to a Whiteley self-portrait and imagines the artist's thoughts and feeling in those last moments and also describes my personal response to the portrait.

Page 16: a relationship breakup; the blues; a guitar

Page 18: Shona words used in this poem are: hasha - anger; chenjera - intelligence; kungura - regret; kurukura - conversation; ndemo mhepo – contrary breeze; manzvinzvidza – shadow. Shona is the native language of Zimbabwe. Written for Peter Roebuck.

Page 20: I often go to the library to write or edit. This little story is written almost exactly as it happened apart from writing in the brother.

Page 22: a love poem that doesn't once use the word "love"

Page 24: the piece is intended to appear almost as a quotation from a longer piece. The line "passing through conversations" is borrowed from a former student, Leigh Hussey, who used it without prior notice in a story he wrote when ten. It has been included as a homage to Leigh, who died far too young.

Page 26: I rarely rhyme poems but did here to appeal to a certain audience. The term "polliegators" is a portmanteau of politician and irrigator and is intended to create a homophonic echo of alligator.

Page 32: Written in the Nobby Pub, north of Warwick. It was a place so fat with characters, I could drink my sundowners there for the rest of my life and never be short of stories.

Page 34: Whilst travelling in north Qld, my wife hurt her back so badly, she had to fly home from Townsville. My conflicting emotions are reflected in those moments watching her plane disappear.

Page 35: Emu Park is a small coastal area north east of Rockhampton. A large sculpture called "the singing ship" sits slightly above the village, facing the Keppel Islands. It has structures which make tuneful noises in the wind. The area was the home of the Darumbul mob but is turned over to tourists now.

Page 36: I have always found Byron pretentious and self indulgent.

Page 38: I love the Tamworth Country Music Festival but in the grip of an Asperger's moment and inspired by "74 denim pockets flapping on thighs", most of this was drafted in a note book whilst have a mocha midst the chaos.

Page 40: this poem is written for two voices and whilst the first four verses are to be said turn about, the fifth verse is to be spoken in alternating unison.

Page 50: this is a real place, in the northern suburbs of Sydney, where I used to meet my psychiatrist. This was my first visit. Flanked on each wall by brilliant bipolars, I felt at home. The receptionist was a casual goth, playing at normality. The last two lines are appropriated from Joni Mitchell's "Turbulent Indigo"

Page 52: just so its clear ... I am a Christian with a strong personal relationship with God. I distrust the church and much of the hypocrisy it systemises but think that some of the best people I have known can be found there, in and out of robes. You won't find me knocking on your door but if you ask, I'll tell you ... but only about me and God. You sort the church out for yourself.

Page 58: The poem is shaped as a challis and the bold letters form a fallen cross

Page 59: "When Dougie Did The Double" is reprinted following it's selection in the SCG "100 Tests Exhibition". Its a favourite. I don't think I've ever performed a reading without using it.

Reader's Notes

A few thanks to those who let me whisper

- Emelia Saban who "discovered" me, told people and then not content, kept telling them. Phar Lap's heart has a challenger;
- Kelly Fuller who has been more than generous of her time and opportunities even though I make her cry;
- Al Rayner, who made me into a Tweater (or is that Twit);
- Sue & Sam for the proof reading (the mistakes are their fault);
- Barry Everingham for keeping a straight face when writing the foreword;
- Sandy McIntosh and his staff at AM Printing for their work and their understanding;
- Jennifer Ingle and all at ABC New England North West;
- Cafe 2340 & Tamworth Regional Library where much of this work was created;
- Glenn Cooper and all at Narnia Bookshop;
- Paul & Jan McManus and all at Collins Bookshop;
- My Dad, whom I love more each year and who has greater perseverance than anyone I have met;
- Rod & Jenny Chiswell for their encouragement;
- Poetzinc (Armidale) for the chance to share my work;
- Tony Bennett for his friendship and the standards he set for me;
- Sam, Sarah & Chris for your love, originality and willingness to keep sharing your lives with me and still call me Dad. You are the bravest people I know;
- The almost impossibly wonderful Sue who is littered with faults that only I know about and is prepared to trust me with the knowledge.